EXPELLED

A Play

Rosalind Butler

WITS UNIVERSITY PRESS

Published in South Africa by:
Wits University Press
1 Jan Smuts Avenue
Johannesburg 2001

www.witspress.co.za

First published 2026

http://dx.doi.org.10.18772/32026091258

978-1-997461-25-8 (Paperback)
978-1-997461-26-5 (Web PDF)
978-1-997461-27-2 (EPUB)

Project manager: Catherine Damerell
Copy editor: Alison Paulin
Proofreader: Christa Büttner-Rohwer
Cover design: Hybrid Creative
Typeset in 10 point Minion Pro

Corrosive and compassionate in equal measure, this compelling three-hander from Rosalind Butler offers its audiences a blistering indictment of contemporary social mores.

— Beverley Brommert, WeekendSpecial

It shocked us, made us laugh, sparked off a fantastic conversation between parent and teen, gave me goosebumps, moved me to tears, got me questioning my own social media addiction, and forced me to answer some uncomfortable questions.

— Shelley Meskin

A spectacularly funny documentary with abundant narrative twists, but in the manner that it turns the lens onto real life, right now, unfolding in real time, it often feels almost excruciatingly close to the bone. … It may just be the year's most hilarious window onto contemporary life, brought to life by three fine actors.

— Keith Bain, *Daily Maverick*

… there are some very cool aspects to the staging, reinforcing a script that amuses in its familiarity as much as it shocks in its reality. All kudos to Rosalind Butler for a play that is very much of our time.

— Karen Rutter, WeekendSpecial

This production is a searing reminder of our current world and reflects on it with razor-sharp wit and intelligence, hilarity and profound truth.

— Sylvaine Strike

I took my Drama students to see it but we should have taken the whole school. It's slick and engaging, calling on adults and teens alike to consider their relationship with social media and with one another.

— Jane Fisher, International School

Contents

Foreword

In a cultural landscape marked by contradiction and deep historical fault lines, we need a range of stories that do not simply reflect our contemporary world but interrogate it. Rosalind Butler's *Expelled* is precisely such a work: bold, incisive, and unafraid to ask difficult questions about privilege and crucibles of power.

At its core, *Expelled* is a family drama set against the backdrop of an elite South African school that is trying to manage a social media crisis. Yet to describe it only in those terms is to understate its reach. Butler deftly situates the intimate dynamics of a single household within a much larger ecosystem – one shaped by an oppressive culture, institutional power and the relentless gaze of social media. What emerges is a toxic cocktail, disturbingly recognisable, in which boyish antics reverberate publicly and where private lives are indistinguishable from the performative spaces we inhabit online.

The play's structure mirrors this fragmentation. Short, punchy scenes unfold over the course of a single week, propelling the narrative with a sense of urgency that feels both theatrical and digital. Interspersed within this dramatic arc are the ever-present images of social media: a world where personal milestones – moving 4D ultrasound images of unborn babies, for instance – are shared alongside cake recipes and millennial lists promising better living. This juxtaposition is intentional. It speaks to a culture in which intimacy is commodified, and where validation is sought not through truth or connection, but through visibility, metrics and the fleeting affirmation of 'likes' and being liked.

From its opening moments, *Expelled* establishes a clear and palpable context. The 'macho' and 'menacing' war cry of the fictional Chiswick high school for boys resounds with unsettling force, immediately immersing us in an elite institutional bubble. This is a world governed by bravado, cut-throat competition and an entrenched patriarchy that confuses dominance with strength. Within this environment, sexism is not an aberration but a norm, sustained through ritual, language and tradition. Reputation becomes currency, and the external markers of belonging – a school tie, a lineage, a network – carry more weight than any genuine measure of character or moral integrity.

Butler's acuity lies in her refusal to render this world in simplistic terms. Instead, she reveals how its values are internalised and perpetuated, often by those who appear, at first glance, to stand apart from it. Lou, Alex's mother, is a particularly compelling example. Initially positioned as an enabler, Lou has assimilated into a culture she at the same time resists, navigating its expectations with a pragmatism that borders on complicity. Her journey forces us to confront uncomfortable questions: to what extent do we become what we tolerate? And how do systems of power sustain themselves through the quiet submission of those within them?

This dynamic finds a powerful echo in the character of Cass, Alex's girlfriend. In the wake of events that have trended online, Cass articulates a contemporary dilemma with piercing clarity: that by remaining in a relationship with Alex, she herself is perceived as complicit – as an enabler of toxicity. In this moment, Butler captures the double bind of modern accountability, where association becomes indictment, and where the court of public opinion renders its judgements swiftly and often without nuance. Cass's predicament underscores one of the play's central tensions: the collision between personal loyalty and public morality in an age where the boundaries between the two have all but dissolved.

In many ways, *Expelled* is a study of bubbles – multiple, overlapping spheres of privilege that insulate their inhabitants from scrutiny while reinforcing a singular worldview. Within these echo chambers, perception eclipses reality, and narratives are shaped less by truth than by the need to maintain a particular image. The school itself is one such bubble, but it is not alone. The characters move through a landscape saturated with other reinforcing influences: the desensitising effects of violent video games, the distortions of pornography and the algorithm-driven feedback loops of social media platforms that reward outrage, spectacle and conformity.

For South African audiences, the resonance of this world is particularly acute. The legacy of elite, patriarchal schooling in this country is deeply entwined with broader histories of exclusion, hierarchy and economic control. Butler's play does not merely critique these traditions; it interrogates how they continue to shape contemporary identities and relationships. It asks us to consider how inherited systems of power persist – not only within institutions, but within the homes, behaviours, expectations and blind spots of individuals who operate inside them.

Yet for all its thematic weight, *Expelled* is far from didactic. One of its most striking qualities is its use of dark, disarming humour. Butler understands that laughter can be a powerful conduit for truth, allowing audiences to lower their defences even as the play's sharper insights take hold. This tonal dexterity ensures that the work remains engaging and accessible, even as it ventures into deeply uncomfortable territory.

Ultimately, *Expelled* does not offer easy answers. It challenges us to examine the values we uphold, the institutions we glorify, and the ways in which we participate, knowingly or otherwise, in elitist cultures that harm as much as they entrench.

Greg Homann
Artistic Director of The Market Theatre
April 2026

Expelled

Expelled was developed as part of the How Now Brown Cow's Writers' Collective. It was first performed at The Baxter Theatre, Cape Town in February 2024, followed by a run at The Market Theatre, Johannesburg in March 2024.

STAGING, CHARACTERS AND SET

The play in one act takes place over one week.
There is no interval.
Warning: graphic content.

Characters on stage

LOU, a woman in her late forties.
RICH, a man in his late forties.
ALEX, a boy of eighteen.

Characters on screen

CASS, a girl of eighteen.
MR MOORE (MOORE in play script),
headmaster, early sixties.

Set

The set is clean and contemporary. There are no walls between the rooms, merely areas that are furnished to create the idea of different rooms. The set is not realistic but has elements that indicate a family home. The walls and floors are white: texts, social media posts and video calls are projected onto the white walls of the set, which double as screens. Scenes that take place in locations other than the family home play downstage, in a neutral, unfurnished space. On stage right, a sofa in neutral colours marks the sitting room area. A narrow daybed is on the other side of the stage, marking Alex's bedroom. A soft curtain conceals the backstage area. As there are no flats with doors between the various 'rooms' on stage, entrances and exits are seamless between these areas. A large tree in a pot is next to the middle exit on the back wall. A curtain hangs across the back exit, which is the only entrance onto and off the stage. This is used only when a character arrives or leaves the house.

SCENE 1

ALEX, *centre stage, takes part in a school rugby war cry. Its macho, menacing tone is heightened. The voices of the war cry leader and the other boys are amplified in the Audio.* ALEX*'s face distorts; the sinews in his neck strain as his testosterone reaches maximum voltage.*

ALEX: Give me a C. Give me an H. Give me an I. Give me an S. Give me a W. Give me an I. Give me a C. Give me a K.

WAR CRY LEADER [*offstage voices*]: What do you get?

ALEX: Chiswick!

WAR CRY LEADER [*offstage voices*]: What do you get?

ALEX: CHISWICK!

The other boys' voices fade away as the lights come up.

LOU *enters from the back entrance and embraces* ALEX.

LOU: You played brilliantly, Lex.

ALEX: I missed that last tackle.

LOU: It's just a game.

ALEX: Not around here.

LOU: When that hulking thug brought you down before half-time, I wanted to run on and slap him.

ALEX: That would have been awkward.

LOU: Do you need some money for tuck?

ALEX: I'm good, thanks, Mom. When will my suit for Cass's dance be ready?

LOU: Half-term.

ALEX: Cool.

LOU: How is Cass?

ALEX: Amazing.

LOU: Send her my love.

ALEX: Sure.

LOU: Quick selfie.

ALEX: Please, no . . .

ALEX *looks around awkwardly, hoping like hell no one is watching.* LOU *holds her phone up.*

LOU: Chin up, bright eyes.

ALEX *raises the phone to get a better selfie angle.* LOU *strikes a pose as she instructed.* ALEX *squints and squirms at the screen.*

LOU: Oh no, my eyes were closed.

LOU *takes another photograph, much to* ALEX'*s irritation.*

ALEX: Please don't post it.

LOU: I won't.

ALEX: Please don't.

LOU: I said I won't.

ALEX: I need to go watch First Team.

They embrace.

LOU: Love you.

ALEX: Love you too.

LOU: See you at half-term. Can't wait.

ALEX [*over his shoulder as he bounds off*]: Mom, do not post it!

> LOU *posts the selfie on Facebook with a large heart emoji; the post is magnified on the screen behind her as the lights fade.*

SCENE 2

LOU *scrolls through Facebook on her iPad on the sofa while* RICH *works on his laptop, seated on a chair in the sitting room area of the set. The light from their screens enhances the light on their faces.*

LOU: Kate's in Greece and Em's in Greece. Separately. Having a lovely time, it seems. Different islands. Different Greek islands. They both keep posting. Kate's breakfast on a hidden beach, Em's sunset at Sunset Bar. No sunrises. Sleeping in, I suppose. Oh, look, Kate's lunch. How delish are these dolmades?

RICH: If they're having such a wonderful time, why do they need to post every two minutes?

LOU: Are they insecure because they post all the time or am I insecure because I look at them and feel dull? [*Beat.*] What's the opposite of exotic?

RICH [*without looking up*]: Dull.

LOU: More than dull. Lacklustre, untanned, un-dolmaded.

RICH: No one's forcing you to look at it.

LOU: Their posts scream 'Look at me living my best life!'

RICH: Block them.

LOU: I can't do that.

RICH: Why not?

LOU: They'll think I don't like them.

RICH: Do you like them?

LOU: Kate's great off Facebook. It's me here and her in Greece I don't like.

LOU *puts her iPad down.*

LOU: I'd like to go somewhere exotic. Maybe Greece. Although between their ten posts a day, I feel I've been there. Croatia? We haven't been anywhere for so long.

RICH: Can't afford to with Alex's school fees.

LOU: If he'd attended our local . . .

RICH: Let's not go there.

LOU: That boat has sailed. That plane has flown without me . . . to Greece.

RICH: Are you okay?

LOU: I think so. What kind of okay?

RICH: You seem a little on edge.

LOU: I need to stop looking at other people's lives. Maybe tomorrow I'll stop. I'll do one of those dramatic 'I am leaving Facebook' announcements. Em did that and an hour later she was back on.

RICH: If the deal comes off, we can go somewhere.

LOU: If . . .

RICH: Why are you so negative? Always so negative.

LOU: Don't want you to be disappointed – again.

RICH: This time is different. I am so close, I can almost smell it.

LOU: What does it smell like?

RICH: Sweet. Very, very sweet.

After a moment, LOU *goes back to her screen.*

LOU: Rachel posted a 4D scan of her baby. A little girl, sacred in her sac beamed to the world. Outed on social media before she is born. Is nothing private anymore?

RICH: Do you have any idea how much you moan about Facebook? Why obsess about something that makes you unhappy?

LOU: Is it Facebook making me unhappy or am I unhappy so I escape into Facebook?

A WhatsApp notification pings on LOU'*s phone.*

LOU [*reading*]: I don't believe it!

RICH: What? Who? How? Who cares?

LOU [*delighted*]: It's from Kate. Em pretended to be in Greece – she was at home the whole time. She used stock pics, made up pithy comments. She was living her best life in PE, not Paros.

RICH: You going to tell her you know?

LOU: No, shame, she's been a little loopy ever since Themba left her and went to live in Mauritius with her younger replacement.

RICH: Does he post Mauritius pics?

LOU: I unfriended him when they split.

RICH: Taking sides?

LOU: You can't be friends with the ex on Facebook. Ever.

RICH: Why not?

LOU: If I liked a pic of Em's nemesis and Em found out, I'd be blocked in real life.

RICH: How desperate do you need to be to fake a holiday?

LOU: If you can pretend to be living the life you want, does that make the life you're not living more real?

RICH: Huh?

LOU: Nothing.

They return to their devices.

LOU: Kate's going for a swim in an infinity pool with a view of the whole bay.

RICH: I honestly don't care what Kate does on her holiday.

LOU: It's John's birthday.

RICH: Shit, better message him.

LOU: No, I'm messaging him now.

RICH: So?

LOU: We can't message him at the same time.

RICH: Why not?

LOU: It'll be obvious I saw it on Facebook and told you.

RICH: You did see it on Facebook and tell me.

LOU: I want him to think I remembered.

RICH: Does it matter?

LOU: Yes.

RICH: So when can I send it?

LOU: About fifteen minutes should be all right.

RICH: Wonderful.

They return to their respective devices. RICH *notices something on his phone.*

RICH: That's strange.

LOU: What?

RICH: There's a missed call from the headmaster.

LOU: Why's he calling?

RICH: Maybe Alex's achieved something at last. Don't they do a final round of prefects around now?

LOU: No, that was first term. Anyway, he doesn't want to be a prefect.

RICH: What does he want? He mooches around aimlessly.

LOU: He works hard.

RICH: No, he doesn't. Year after year at prize giving, we watch other kids swamped with certificates, medals, trophies, while Alex sits in the clearly labelled non-prizewinners section.

LOU: Poor Alex. They might as well brand loser on their foreheads.

RICH: If poor Alex did some actual work, he could be up there, too.

LOU: Not everyone can get six distinctions.

RICH: He could do better, Lou, and you know it.

LOU: He wants to get out of there.

RICH: He doesn't understand what it means.

LOU: What does it mean?

RICH: He's set up for life. He knows people who are connected. In most places, the old school tie gets you in the door.

LOU: You imagine your tie has all this power, your sword that will hack through life's obstacles.

RICH: It's a fact, we Chiswick boys are hugely successful.

LOU: Mmmm, you're confident enough to push to the front of the queue. Not Alex though, he's different.

RICH: Alex doesn't even join the queue.

LOU: In a few months he will be free, everything will open up for him.

RICH: If he gets decent marks. If.

LOU: He might surprise you.

RICH: No.

LOU: You should call him back.

RICH: Who?

LOU: Mr Moore.

RICH: Oh right, mmm.

RICH *changes his persona when he talks to the headmaster, almost as if he were back at school and eager to please.*

RICH: Mr Moore, Richard Bolton here, sorry I missed your call. How are you?

Pause as RICH *listens.*

RICH: Yes. Tomorrow? Um, yes, we could get there by then. Any reason why? No, of course. See you then.

RICH *hangs up, perturbed.*

LOU: What?

RICH: Emergency meeting tomorrow.

LOU: About what?

RICH: He wouldn't say. Just said he needs to see us. Urgently. Did Alex say anything about anything?

LOU: No, nothing.

RICH: Moore was a bit off. Strange, isn't it?

LOU: Yes.

RICH [*concerned*]: Alex wouldn't get into trouble, would he?

LOU: No. Not Alex. Never.

Lights down.

SCENE 3

The pure and angelic sounds of boys singing 'Amazing Grace' fill the space. A projection of a stained glass window on the back wall creates a chapel effect. ALEX, *in a pool of light, sings. He surreptitiously gets his buzzing phone out of his pocket. As he looks at the texts, the exchange is visible.* ALEX *replies furtively while still pretending to sing.*

BOYS [*singing*]: 'Amazing Grace, how sweet the sound that saved a wretch like me. I once was lost but now am found, was blind, but now I see.'

The texts between AYANDA *and* ALEX *appear on the screen as* ALEX *types.*

AYANDA: They've called our rents up for a special meeting.
ALEX: You're not serious? When?
AYANDA: Tomorrow.
ALEX: Fuck.
AYANDA: Right.
ALEX: How did they find out?
AYANDA: TJ shared it with the teachers.
ALEX: What a dick.
AYANDA: Total.
ALEX: Why would he do that?
AYANDA: Fuck knows.
ALEX: Jesus.
BOYS: 'Twas grace that taught my heart to fear, and grace my fears relieved . . .'

Lights down as the music fades.

SCENE 4

Lights up on the sitting room. Enraged RICH *and stunned* LOU *face* ALEX.

RICH: Are you going to say anything about this? You sat in the car on your phone for two hours.

ALEX: I don't know what to say.

RICH: Do you know what a colossal fuck-up this is?

LOU: Language. Please.

RICH: Oh, come on, it's not like he doesn't use it. Not your innocent little boy anymore, Lou. Far fucking from it.

ALEX [*mumbling*]: I'm sorry.

RICH: Sorry?

ALEX: Yes. Sorry.

RICH: Wow. Sorry?

LOU: Rich . . .

RICH: Sorry Dad, you sent me to one of the most expensive schools and I fucked it up. Sorry you've sucked up to your boss for years, let him win every round of golf so you could afford to pay the school fees, for me to fuck it up. Sorry you gave me every chance you could imagine and I fucked it all up spectacularly. Is that what you're sorry for? Is it?

LOU: Rich, please . . .

ALEX: Yes.

RICH: Well, I do not accept your sorry. Do you get that? Do you?

RICH *grabs* ALEX.

LOU: Leave him, let him go, if you hurt him . . .

RICH *shoves* ALEX *roughly.* ALEX *staggers backwards.*

RICH: Get out!

LOU: Richard, that's enough.

RICH: I haven't even started.

ALEX *leaves the room.*

RICH [*pacing*]: Fuck. Fuuuuuuccccck!

LOU: What are we going to do?

RICH: I don't know. Has there been anything from the school?

LOU: They sent a newsletter detailing the unfortunate incident. They don't mention names.

RICH: Their faces are all over it. No need to guess who they are. Idiots! How dense can you be?

LOU: They are just boys.

RICH: I mean to film it, to post it! Fuuuuucking hell!

LOU: Everyone must be talking about it.

RICH: When you say everyone, you don't mean everyone. I don't think people in Bangladesh are banging on about it, are they?

LOU: If you know what I mean, why do you need to snip.

RICH: Strangely I'm feeling very, very snippy!

LOU: Why would Alex get mixed up in something like that?

RICH: You've always been too soft on him.

LOU: Don't make this about me. Before social media, generations of boys did silly things, and their lives weren't destroyed. I'm going to ask Mr Moore to be lenient.

RICH: The school will sort it out, they have their discipline procedures.

LOU: They don't understand social media or how fast it can unravel.

LOU's *phone beeps with a message notification.*

LOU [*reading*]: Kerry. Are you okay? XXX.

RICH: If Kerry knows, we're fucked.

SCENE 5

ALEX *is on a video call to* CASS. *Her filmed side of the call is projected onto the wall opposite him. He talks directly to her on the screen.*

CASS: Hey, I miss you.

ALEX: Miss you too. The rents are out of control. Like insane. The way everyone's carrying on, you'd think we'd killed someone. Hopefully they'll all calm the fuck down.

CASS: Do you think you'll be back in time for the dance?

ALEX: Even if I'm not back at school, I can still come.

CASS: Be better if you were back.

ALEX: Have you seen the clip?

CASS: Don't want to. Liyema says if we're going to stay together, I'd better not.

ALEX: Thanks, Liyema.

CASS: She says it's SO bad.

ALEX: It wasn't meant to have an audience.

CASS: Can you believe it, Hales is organising a march to Chiswick?

ALEX: What the fuck! Why?

CASS: You know how she is. She says the video is proof, what did she say? Proof of the toxic masculinity embedded in every brick of the school.

ALEX: Can everyone just calm down?

CASS: I told her, Alex is not like that, whatever. Apparently, I buy into the toxicity. I'm an enabler.

ALEX: Bullshit.

CASS: I was like, whatever, Hales. She is unbelievable.

ALEX: I think of you all the time.

CASS [*smiling*]: No, you don't. Not all the time.

ALEX: All the time. Don't you want to take your top off?

CASS: I can't now.

ALEX: Why?

CASS: Got an extra maths lesson in five.

ALEX: You can take it off in one.

CASS: Not now, babe. Got to go.

ALEX: Later?

CASS: Maybe.

CASS *blows a kiss and cuts the call.*

SCENE 6

LOU *scrolls mindlessly on her iPad. A series of images, loosely related to what she says she is seeing, scroll rapidly over one of the walls of the set.*

LOU: I scroll and I scroll and I scroll – looking for something. Not sure what I'm searching for. Plum cheesecake? Should I make it? So many ingredients. All that sugar. On I go, on and on. I don't find it, that thing, that morsel of meaning whispering to me beyond the screen: I am in here somewhere . . . come on, wade through the endless nothingness, the fury, the rage, the pride. Look at me, no look at me. What about me? And me?

LOU *stands and scrolls with exaggerated arm movements, as if conducting an orchestra. The images multiply and now surround her on all the walls, as if consuming her.*

LOU: I scroll on, my fingers become graceful, an upward movement, up, up, up, like a conductor, the Facebook symphony – Meaningless in A Minor. I have so much to do, but I can't stop. It must be in here somewhere. A way to ease the burden of being? Eighteen behaviours of emotionally intelligent people. Foreigners hacked to death in Baghdad, or six of the best diet tips ever. Someone's dead mum's birthday, they still miss them. Ah, a quote. Take a breath and look around you.

LOU *does as instructed and looks around the room.*

SCENE 6

LOU: The curtain hem is coming out. Which reminds me, the hall rug needs dry cleaning.

ALEX *enters.*

ALEX: Ma, is there anything to eat?

LOU: Yes, it's in that place called the fridge.

Beat.

ALEX: Mom, say I am expelled.

LOU: Please, no.

ALEX: Just say I am.

LOU: Yes.

ALEX: Finals are three months away. What'll happen?

LOU: Maybe you should have thought about that before that video.

ALEX: We didn't know it would go viral.

LOU: So the sharing is the problem?

ALEX: No! I'm not saying that.

LOU: What are you saying?

ALEX: We were bored, messing around, Sunday after chapel. Just a stupid moment, I mean, we had no idea it would be seen.

LOU: For goodness' sake, someone must have been filming.

ALEX: Ayanda is always filming everything; he calls it the record of his amazing life. He sent it to a closed group of other Chiswick guys. Most of them thought it was hilarious, but then TJ saw it. His sister was raped – like in real life. He was triggered and sent it to everyone he knows. Once it was out there, it was game over.

LOU: Do you know why Mrs Moore has a wig?

ALEX: No.

LOU: She has stage three breast cancer. She's having chemo. The dressing gown is in case she vomits while enduring twelve hours of poison. The wig is also a spare; her hair's fallen out, and she has little tufts left like a newborn chicken.

ALEX: How do you know this?

LOU: I called her to apologise on your behalf.

ALEX: I didn't know she had cancer.

LOU: She wanted to battle it out in private. That choice has been taken away because you and your horrendous friends . . .

ALEX: They're just guys I hang out with. Ayanda's the only one I like.

LOU: Is that honestly how you see women? Receptacles?

ALEX: Come on, Ma.

LOU: I saw it. I sat with the headmaster, watching my son encouraging other idiots pretending to be the headmaster, raping his wife. Do you have any idea what that was like, Alex?

ALEX: That's not what we were doing.

LOU: That's what it looks like!

ALEX: I'm sorry . . . it was . . .

LOU: I saw a statistic the other day, someone shared it somewhere, maybe Facebook – a woman is raped every second of every day, worldwide. Right now, many, many women are being violently forced to have sex.

ALEX: We didn't rape anyone. Everyone's acting like we did something real, like actually hurt someone. No one was raped in that video.

LOU: You were clapping and laughing while watching a mock rape.

ALEX: We were just having a laugh.

LOU: Rape is not funny, Alex. It's never funny.

ALEX: We were fooling around, being dumb, that's all it would have been if Ayanda hadn't filmed it. We were bored, you have no idea how bored you can get there. Anything for a laugh. I get that it was stupid and like . . . offensive. But Timothy in that dress and the wig, and Barker . . . in the moment . . . it was funny. But because other people saw it, there's this . . . like . . . that's who we are, that's all we are . . . and we're not, not even Barker. No, okay, Barker really is that kind of guy, but the rest of us . . . we're not those guys.

Beat.

LOU: When you were a baby, you'd laugh in your sleep. I would feed you, you'd fall asleep in my arms, and laugh, this hearty little chuckle. Pure joy, the sweetest sound I'd ever heard. What happened to that perfect little boy?

ALEX: No one's perfect, Ma.

ALEX *walks out.*

SCENE 7

RICH *walks downstage and talks directly to the audience.*

RICH: When I walked into the club this afternoon, I could have sworn people were avoiding me. I was a bit nervous about seeing the boss, Phillips, being an old boy and all that. He was fine though – boys will be boys was his take.

Further upstage, on the sofa, LOU *scrolls on her iPad. Neither refers to the other; they are in separate spaces, in their own worlds.*

LOU: On I go, up and up and up and up. Best ever shampoo. Cottage to rent. Trapped in the classifieds, but on I go. Ava turned five. Love this child. Thank goodness, she *is* yours.

RICH: Barker's threatening to sue the school, not sure what for? We can commiserate at the next meeting, chat about our naughty boys as we iron out the final details before signing the deal.

LOU: Oh no, Mira's mother was attacked in her house. God.

LOU *types a response.*

LOU: So sorry. Wishing her a swift recovery. [*Beat.*] Care emoji? Or heart rather? No, then it will seem I love it. Angry perhaps? No, no. Care emoji.

Satisfied with her choice, LOU *posts her response.*

LOU: These comments . . . [*reading*] 'What is happening to this country?', 'So pleased I live in Australia'. Reply to

Oz is Paradise comment: 'My sister-in-law's cousin's wife was attacked in Perth and left for dead. Just saying'. A few 'no words'. Does saying no words mean more than simply no words at all? 'No words' is actually two words. No. Words. Is it, I'm speechless? This is beyond expressing. I cannot think of a single word. Not even fuck.

RICH: Phillips said the school board is going to be hard-line with the boys. He thinks they'll be officially out within a week.

LOU: Sadfishing all over my feed this morning. Simone was banned from her daughter's wedding, now she's expressing her pain, raw and intimate. What time did she post? Oh yes, late last night, a bottle or two in. A couple of cares, a few loves, but no likes and no comments. Should I tell her Facebook is not therapy, Simone? It's the wrong platform, darling. Or rather, no words.

RICH: I wonder if you get the deposit back if your son's expelled.

Lights down.

SCENE 8

LOU *walks across to* ALEX.

LOU: Did you see the email?

ALEX: From who?

LOU: The school.

ALEX: What did it say?

LOU: Do you ever check your email?

ALEX [*shrugging*]: Email's not really a thing, Mom. What's it about?

LOU: You must apologise to the headmaster and his wife at a special assembly.

ALEX: I wrote to them saying sorry.

LOU: This is a formal apology in front of the entire school community.

ALEX: How many times do they want me to apologise? A thousand? Ten thousand?

LOU: As many as it takes. Even then, some things you can't take back. It's out there. Right now, someone is probably watching it. You will do whatever, beg, grovel, plead . . . whatever it takes to salvage your future!

LOU *exits.*

ALEX, *straight to the audience, practises his apology.*

ALEX: I am sorry, really sorry, Mrs Moore, we had no idea you were, you know, like not well.

Beat.

ALEX: Sick maybe? Naah, that sounds kak. Please accept my apology for any harm done to you personally or to Chiswick.

ALEX *groans; he finds the idea of apologising publicly excruciating.*

ALEX: I feel so bad. My bad. All bad. We messed up – big time. So sorry a million, billion times but . . . let's be honest here. This was no big deal compared to what really goes down in the hallowed halls of college. If we are going to talk about respecting women? You guys literally have no idea what gets said every day.

Lights down.

SCENE 9

LOU, *with her computer in front of her, nervously addresses the headmaster on a Zoom call.* MOORE, *filmed in a Zoom call format, is projected onto one side wall, taking up the entire wall.*

LOU: Mr Moore, I'm so sorry to hear about Mrs Moore's diagnosis.

MOORE: You're muted, Mrs Bolton.

LOU: Sorry?

MOORE: You're muted, Mrs Bolton.

LOU: Oh gosh.

LOU *unmutes herself.*

LOU: I was saying how sorry I am about your wife's illness. I . . . I can't imagine what you've been going through. We're deeply sorry you were mocked like that. So ashamed that Alex was involved.

MOORE *nods, unmoved.*

LOU: I understand there must be some kind of punishment, but I hope it will be fair.

MOORE: What would you consider fair, Mrs Bolton?

LOU: Some kind of community service, perhaps? They have no idea how lethal social media can be. I'm not sure any of us understand its power, but they're just foolish boys being foolish.

MOORE: I don't think mocking me raping my wife can be written off as foolish.

LOU: If only it had been another teacher.

MOORE: I'm not sure that's the point. Alex would be dealt with in the same way, no matter who the teacher was.

LOU: Right. But it is personal for you.

MOORE: When you face the death of the woman you love, nothing else matters all that much.

LOU: How is Mrs Moore?

MOORE: Surviving.

LOU: This is awfully awful on every level, but please . . . be gentle with them. Alex is just a boy, my boy. A sweet, silly boy. He laughed, that's all he did, he didn't steal the clothes from your car or simulate rape. He laughed.

MOORE: And clapped. Practically cheered.

LOU: That's not who he is. Teenage boys are a mass of hormones; they don't understand consequences. Their frontal cortexes aren't properly developed. They only develop fully at twenty-five. That's a fact. You can look it up on the internet.

MOORE: I'm aware of the development of the frontal cortex, Mrs Bolton.

LOU: Of course you are. Sorry.

MOORE: The school's reputation is taking a battering. Chiswick is trending for all the wrong reasons.

LOU: These things die down; people move on to the next sensation or scandal.

MOORE: This needs to be dealt with in a way that pleases the parents, and indeed the entire Chiswick community, and appeases the press.

LOU: And fuck the rest! Sorry, sorry, I didn't mean to swear. I never normally swear but honestly, this is such a fuck-up!

The projection of MOORE's *side of the call snaps off abruptly.*

RICH *walks in and notes* LOU *in a funk.*

RICH: You okay?

LOU: I had a meeting with Mr Moore.

RICH [*stunned*]: You drove all the way to Chiswick?

LOU: Zoom. It was a Zoom meeting.

RICH: Why did you do that?

LOU: I had to do something. What are you doing?

RICH: Mommy running to beg for special favours for her little boy makes us look pathetic.

LOU: Alex's life cannot be ruined by one moment of bad judgement. I won't allow it.

RICH: What did Moore say?

LOU: He claims the hearing will be fair. I think it's a formality. They've made up their minds.

RICH: So that's it. It will be as if he never went there. All that money wasted.

LOU: Boarding school wasn't right for him. I knew it. I gave in to you. I let him go . . .

RICH: Oh, please, you loved it when we went for the open day. You went on and on. They were so welcoming. The grounds were astounding, the endless fields, the magnificent view, even the snacks met with your approval.

LOU: It was impressive. But you knew what lay beneath the surface and you still sent him there, a shy, gentle thirteen-year-old. When Alex phoned us crying every night in his first year, we should have pulled him out.

RICH: He never tried to fit in. He did his best to be averagely average.

LOU: What if that's who he is? Average.

RICH: He could be more, way more. Not now. Not anymore.

LOU: I never fitted in there either. All those rich parents wearing their wealth as if they owned it.

RICH: They do own it. They earned it. They made it. You don't like successful people because . . .

Beat. RICH *manages to stop himself from saying what he was about to say.*

LOU: Because what?

RICH: Never mind.

LOU: Because I'm unsuccessful? You're right. Aborted career. Cracked marriage. I thought I was a good mother, but I clearly failed in that, too.

RICH: You were a good mother.

LOU: Were?

RICH: Are! There is nothing you could have done to stop this.

LOU: If there was, I would have, you know that.

RICH: I know.

Beat.

RICH: There are plenty of warm, kind, generous people who send their children to Chiswick. We had that fantastic week away at the Akbars' private game reserve – plunge pool . . . Never get invited there again.

LOU: All you've talked about is what people will think.

RICH: That is of huge concern.

LOU: And your son spurring on a mock rape is not?

RICH: Well, obviously it is.

LOU: Alex's first experience of sex was pornography on your computer. When he was eight, he was looking at animals starting with B. We didn't get to buck or bunny because he typed beaver . . . up it popped. Filling the screen. What kind of beaver is this, Mom? I leapt across the room like a professional pole vaulter and shut it down. 'Just a silly photograph, let's find some bunnies.' Just saying, Rich.

SCENE 10

Seated on his bed, ALEX *plays a violent video game, wearing gaming headphones. The game's sound effects are amplified, and the blurry game visuals surround him on all the walls.*

ALEX [*quietly*]: Hey, there are two cubs, so sick. That other guy's gone. Just wait . . . he's stuck his head out of the trench. He's right there, behind you. Turn slowly. Do you see him? Behind the cubs. He's watching you. Have you got him? [*shouting*] Fucker! He's there! [*manically*] Okay . . . shoot! Kill him. Fuck! You missed, arsehole. Aaahh, now he's shot me! Why don't you aim properly? Fall back. Where did he go? He's there. Shoot now! I told you to shoot. [*screaming, deranged*] Shoot now! Kill him! Motherfucker!

ALEX *loses it, the headphones go flying, he smashes a pillow on his bed. The words GAME OVER are projected on all the walls of the set.* ALEX *tries to pull himself together. He picks up the headphones.*

ALEX: Sorry, bro, lost it there a bit. Taking heavy fire with the rents. This fucking thing. I just want it to be over.

SCENE 11

LOU *breaks the fourth wall and talks to the audience, almost taking them into her confidence. No images are shown during her monologue.*

LOU: I try to scroll as fast as my fingers can move, avoiding the boasts, the banal, the boring. Sight versus sound, the fragments reach your brain at the speed of light, and in that nanosecond, you receive 'she cried through the five-year-old's adorable dragon concert'. That riveting information has travelled deep into my brain and might take up precious space forever.

What if the place in your brain where memories are captured has limited bandwidth? What if the 'adorable dragon concert' replaces Alex when he was three, in his Ben 10 t-shirt, squeezing my cheeks with his pudgy little fingers, saying 'I love you, Mama'? What if that's erased like emails when your mailbox is full? Out with a memory I love and in with a stranger's experience. One day, I'll think it was adorable Alex swishing his dragon tail.

Maybe news sites are better. [*reading*] Teenager marries dead boyfriend in a coffin. How does that work? Who says 'I do' for him? Maybe they use reverb to make it sound like a voice from the dead. I doooooooooo! What if he didn't want to get married? What if he was a commitment-phobe but now, like it or not, he's married. Do the dead have no rights? A dead husband.

SCENE 11

LOU *looks at* RICH, *who is lost in his phone.*

RICH: What's that?
LOU: Nothing.

The lights from their sitting room dim.

SCENE 12

ALEX *is on a video call with* CASS. CASS's *side of the call is projected onto one side wall.* ALEX *sits on his bed, facing her as he talks to her enlarged image.*

ALEX: Hopefully, I'll be back at school before the dance.
CASS: [*awkwardly*]: I need to talk to you about that.
ALEX: I can't change the colour of my suit!
CASS: It's not that. Listen, I can't take you.
ALEX: What?
CASS: My father says you've destroyed Chiswick's reputation.
ALEX: Are you serious?
CASS: Ja.
ALEX [*stunned*]: Who are you going to take, then?
CASS: I don't know.
ALEX: You do.

Beat.

ALEX: Who? Tell me. Come on.
CASS: Dylan.
ALEX: Dylan Vermeulen?
CASS: Yes.
ALEX: He's an idiot, arrogant, racist.
CASS: Please don't do this.
ALEX: Are you into him?
CASS: No! Alex, we can't carry on.
ALEX: Are you breaking up with me?
CASS: You haven't given me a choice.
ALEX: You serious? Is your father forcing you?

CASS: No.

ALEX: Then why?

CASS: I can't, not after . . . you're all cancelled, Alex.

ALEX: Wow. Fuck. Wow.

CASS: Sorry.

ALEX: Please don't do this.

CASS: I do love you.

ALEX: But not enough to stay with me?

CASS: I must go.

ALEX: Please don't go.

CASS: Chapel is in half an hour.

ALEX: Take off your top.

CASS: We're not doing this anymore. It's over.

ALEX: One last time.

CASS: No. No.

ALEX: Please.

CASS: Don't you get no, Alex? Clearly not. 'You say no, but you mean yes.'

ALEX: You watched it?

CASS: Come on, everyone's watched it.

ALEX: You know I'm not like that, I would never force anyone to do anything; I get consent.

CASS: But you want me to take my top off?

ALEX: You sent me the first nude, I didn't ask you . . . what are you saying?

CASS: Delete everything I sent you. All those pics. Will you?

Beat.

CASS: Will you? Will you?

ALEX: Okay.
CASS: Promise?
ALEX: Promise.

Beat.

CASS: Bye, Alex.
ALEX: Wait . . .

CASS *exits the call and the screen goes black.*

ALEX: Fuck!

SCENE 13

LOU *and* RICH *appear more relaxed with one another in the sitting room area.*

RICH: Still nothing about the date for the hearing?

LOU: Why are they taking so long? It's not even being shared much anymore.

RICH: The press have latched onto it, there's a fresh wave of outrage. Now they're gunning for the school.

LOU: I wish they'd drop the guillotine so we can find a place for Alex to write finals.

RICH: This will follow Alex around like a bad smell. Roger Milton, in my year, was expelled for stealing. He was forty, and people still mentioned it every time his name came up. Never really amounted to anything. Gassed himself in a garage in Norway eventually.

LOU: So depressing, I can't bear it.

LOU *picks up her iPad.* RICH *looks at his iPad, each escaping to their other worlds.*

RICH: Rassie thinks we can win the World Cup three times in a row. What a guy.

LOU [*reading*]: Famous celebrities' deaths, which one would you choose?

RICH: You can't choose your death, unless you orchestrate it, like poor old Milton.

LOU: I think I'd choose Steve Jobs' passing. Seconds before he went, he said 'Wow, wow, wow'. Wonder what he saw? Must have been beautiful.

RICH: That was a lack of oxygen, euphoria.

LOU: I'd rather see it as heaven.

RICH: There is no heaven.

LOU: There certainly is hell – on earth. Bombs, dead babies, senseless wars. Maybe Facebook is hell and no one has told us.

RICH: Hell's not voluntary.

LOU: Facebook's a torrent of lava devouring my brain.

RICH: You don't have to carry on clicking, you know.

LOU: I'm like a zombie, that's all I can do – click, click, click.

RICH: You live there more than you do here.

LOU: At least I'm alive somewhere.

RICH: You claim you hate Facebook, but whenever I say anything slightly critical, you get so defensive.

LOU: It's love–hate, a bit like a marriage, really.

RICH: When do I get to feel the love part?

LOU: Hopefully it's there, hidden, lurking, dazed and confused. Maybe one day it'll pop out again and say hello, you two, I'm back.

For a moment they look at one another, as if they could connect, but neither can bridge the chasm.

RICH: I'd better go. I shouldn't be back too late.

LOU: Where are you going?

RICH: Barker wants to fine-tune the last details of the deal.

LOU: Great, so none of this has affected anything?

RICH: No.

RICH *exits.*

LOU [*as an afterthought*]: Good luck!

SCENE 14

LOU *enters* ALEX's *room. She sits on his bed.*

ALEX: Sizwe the cleaner's been fired. Moore found out he bought us beers on the day, that day.

LOU: He bought you beers?

ALEX: Barker practically forced him.

LOU: Drinking at school? Why?

ALEX: Lots of guys drink. Only at weekends.

LOU: As if that makes it better. You could have been expelled for *that.*

ALEX: It was just beers. Connor has a case of vodka stashed in the store cupboard.

LOU: Is there anything else you'd like to tell me? Get it all out, let's go full disclosure.

ALEX: No, that's it. Promise.

LOU *sighs.*

ALEX: Sizwe supports his sister, he needs the job, this isn't fair.

LOU: Tell Jules Barker to tell Mr Moore this was his fault.

ALEX: Barker is a pathological liar; he doesn't care.

LOU: Maybe we can give Sizwe some money until he finds a new job?

ALEX: We've destroyed his life. Why is this happening?

LOU: It will end, it must end.

ALEX: What if my marks aren't good enough to get into university?

LOU: You can rewrite finals next year.

ALEX: No, no, I need to be in the same uni year as Cass. It's the only thing that's keeping me going.

LOU's *desperation for her child surges.*

LOU: I can get you a tutor, whatever you need. I will be here, helping you get through this. Gran said to tell you anyone can make a mistake, it's what you do afterwards that counts.

SCENE 15

LOU *enters from another part of the house as upbeat* RICH *enters from outside.*

RICH: Excellent meeting. We are days away from signing. This is it. The big time, baby!

LOU: Great. There's a casserole in the oven. Kerry brought it, like someone died.

RICH: I'll eat later.

Beat.

RICH: You look pretty.

LOU [*surprised*]: Really? Thanks.

RICH *hands* LOU *some brochures.*

LOU: What are these?

RICH: Places where Alex can write matric next year. Colleges.

LOU: He hasn't been expelled yet.

RICH: I think he will be. He can finish at one of these places. Maybe we can move. To the Cape. Stellenbosch. Somerset West?

LOU: What's brought this on?

RICH: A change might be exactly what we need.

LOU: What's happened to you?

RICH: Nothing.

LOU: You're all . . . perky.

RICH: Perky? I wouldn't say perky.

LOU: What would you say?

RICH: Definitely not perky.

RICH *looks away, keen to change the subject.*

RICH: What's for supper?

LOU: I told you, Kerry's casserole's in the oven.

RICH: Oh yes, right.

LOU: Why are you so odd? Was it the meeting?

RICH: The meeting was . . . interesting.

LOU: Why?

RICH: Barker's not going to sue the school anymore. He knew he didn't stand a chance. He's got a new plan now.

LOU: What plan?

RICH *knows it will not get a positive reaction.*

LOU: What plan does he have?

LOU *stares* RICH *down, forcing it out of him.*

RICH: He wants Alex to say he took the bag with Mrs Moore's things from the car, forced them all to do it, basically exonerate his son.

LOU: What a disgusting thing to ask. He is as vile as his offspring. You told him to eff off? Right?

Beat.

LOU: You didn't say yes, did you? You wouldn't do that. Would you?

RICH: If I don't, he will shaft me out of the deal.

LOU [*shocked*]: He's playing you.

RICH: He knows how much I need this.

LOU: It's not worth it.

RICH: Our overdraft is off the chart. If this deal falls through, we are finished. I put three million into it, took it out of the bond.

LOU: What?

RICH: I had to. I need this. We need this. If it bombs, I'm dead.

LOU: We'll make a plan.

RICH: Easy for you to say, you haven't earned anything for eighteen years.

LOU: You didn't want Alex to have a mother who worked.

RICH: You could have gone back when he went to college.

LOU: It was too late.

RICH: You didn't even try.

LOU: I was behind on the software, the systems, everyone I'd worked with had moved on.

RICH: If this falls through, we will have to sell the house.

LOU: I'd rather live in a flat than you do this to Alex.

RICH: It won't make any difference to the outcome.

LOU: Alex – the ringleader? Moore will never buy it.

RICH: I won't let him destroy years of work, days before it pays off.

LOU: Is this who you are? The father who forces his son to lie?

RICH: It's his fault Barker has leverage over me.

LOU: If you do this, I'll leave you.

RICH: Finally you will have your excuse.

LOU: Do you ever wonder why things are so bad?

RICH: Yes, of course I do, as I lie there, night after night, next to you, there might as well be an ocean between us. Sexless islands of humanity.

LOU: I'm not the only one with an online life.

RICH: What does that mean?

LOU: I know what you do when you think I'm asleep, salivating over your screen. I looked at your search history, endless sites . . .

RICH: What am I supposed to do if my wife won't sleep with me?

LOU *doesn't want to go there.*

LOU: Asking Alex to lie is the worst thing you can do.

RICH: He owes me.

LOU: Did he ask to go to Chiswick?

RICH: This is between me and my son. He is my son, too, Lou, something you seem to forget.

LOU: Please?

RICH: Stay out of it.

RICH *turns to leave.*

LOU [*shouting after him*]: He will say no!

RICH: Stay out of it!

SCENE 16

ALEX *is listening to something on his headphones and, at first, doesn't notice his father entering.* RICH *makes his presence known.* ALEX *removes the headphones, surprised to see his father there.*

RICH [*awkwardly*]: How are you doing?

ALEX [*hesitantly*]: Fine, thanks, and you?

RICH: Fine.

Beat. ALEX *is unsure about why his father is there.*

RICH: What if you left Barker out of it?

ALEX [*confused*]: What do you mean?

RICH: His father is keen for him to be removed from the equation.

ALEX: Barker stole the bag of Mrs Moore's stuff from the head's car, he wanted exam papers but then he found it . . .

RICH: Alex, this commercial property sale I've been working on is in the balance. His father can kill it, if he wants to.

ALEX: What are you saying, Dad?

RICH: Just hear me out. If you could say you took the bag from the car and forced Barker to take part in the . . . whatever that was.

ALEX [*amazed*]: Are you selling me out, Dad?

RICH: No, just . . .

ALEX [*matter of fact*]: Selling me out.

RICH: I'm in a tight corner, my boy.

ALEX: Why should Barker get off?

RICH: Because his father has the power to push me out of the sale, which we need, really, really need. Whatever way you leave Chiswick, it won't be what I wanted.

ALEX: What did you want, Dad? Me to be someone else?

RICH: No.

ALEX: Then what?

RICH *sits next to* ALEX.

RICH: I wanted it to be different for you.

ALEX: How could it be different? It's the same school you went to.

RICH: You weren't a charity case like me.

ALEX [*confused*]: What do you mean?

RICH: I got a bursary to Chiswick. I tried to fit in. Adopt the casualness of the wealthy. I told them all my father was a lawyer working for the UN. They bought it until the end of the first year. Parents' cocktail party. My errant father decided to pitch up and lurch in. Hadn't seen him in about four years. For a second, I was happy – my Dad's here. He shouted across the quad – 'There's my boy, Richie Rich'. He downed a drink, not his first. Free booze, why not make the most of it? His hair was greasy, shoes scuffed, no tie, no suit. I walked over to him. I quietly begged him to leave. He shouted to people avoiding him, 'My son's trying to throw me out of his posh school'. Downed a few more glasses. Other boys watched, sniggering. Millard laughed so hard it looked like he was crying. My father got louder, more insulting. Until, slurring, he spilt his drink over the chairman's suit. He was thrown out. I never saw him again. Your grandfather. After that, no one called me Richard or Bolton, it was Hobo Junior till I left. I pretended to find it hilarious. As if I didn't care. But I cared. I swore my son would be a full-fee paying kid. Be everything I'd wanted. I'd stand on the side of the field with the other first-team parents, 'There, that's my boy, the one scoring the try, that's him, that's my boy. Go, my boy! You go, boy! You go, my boy.'

SCENE 17

LOU *approaches* ALEX *tentatively.*

LOU: Did your Dad . . . ?

ALEX: Yip.

LOU: You didn't agree, did you?

ALEX: I might as well do something to make Dad proud.

LOU: Is that what he said?

ALEX: He didn't have to. He's always had this low-grade disappointment with me. Never quite good enough. Never the best.

LOU: There is so much that lies ahead for you. Don't do this.

ALEX: Just feels like everything is closing in on me. I don't even know who I am anymore.

LOU: I do. You're kind and brave. You stuck it out at school and forged a way through. You're an intelligent, empathetic, decent human being.

ALEX: I'm not, I'm a fuck-up.

LOU: Don't say that, it's not true.

ALEX: Cass broke up with me.

LOU: No! Oh my baby, I am so sorry.

ALEX: She's taking Dylan Vermeulen to the dance.

LOU: You're joking!

ALEX: Dylan! Dylan? Like Dylan, what the fuck? Sorry, I know you hate it when I swear.

LOU: It's okay. Sometimes swearing is . . . therapeutic. You're not a fuck-up. Far from it.

ALEX: I'll be expelled whether I do this for Dad or not.

LOU: You're better than this.

ALEX: You just think that because I'm your kid.

LOU: If you can't see how special you are, I've failed you as a mother.

Mother and son embrace one another fiercely.

ALEX: You're the best mom, I love you so much.

LOU: I love you beyond time and space.

LOU *and* ALEX *continue to hold one another.*

LOU: Cass can go to hell! She doesn't deserve you!

ALEX: Ma, you're so extra.

RICH *enters, he avoids looking at* LOU.

RICH: Alex, we need to go.

ALEX *exits.*

LOU: Richard, don't do this.

RICH: This will save us from losing everything.

LOU: Let's lose it all.

RICH: Be real, Lou, for once.

LOU: Please, please . . . you don't see what you are doing.

RICH: Can't you see what he has done?

LOU: He's a child.

RICH: He's eighteen. He can vote and drive.

LOU: I cannot tell you how much I hate you right now.

ALEX *enters, carrying his school uniform.*

RICH: Alex, let's go.

RICH *and* ALEX *leave as* LOU *watches helplessly. The lights dim.* LOU *turns to the audience and addresses them directly.*

LOU: I was trying to avoid the posts I hate, like six cute child stars who turned into ugly adults, or the ten richest families in the world. I finished looking at eight new looks for sitting rooms, and there was Jasmine's post. With Oscar Pistorius's release, things are coming up again. I block people who post photos of dead people. Anyone who shared that the refugee baby drowned in the waves – blocked. I don't want to see dead people on Facebook. I want to see decor, health tips, and what my ex-boyfriend from high school is doing. I opened the link . . . without thinking. It even had a warning – graphic content. I clicked, almost in a trance, until there she was. Reeva – clearly dead. Blue lips dead but still beautiful. So beautiful. I shut it down immediately, blocked Jasmine, but that image is still in my mind. Four bullets later, bruised, mottled, pale, broken, blue and beautiful. Still so beautiful.

SCENE 18

RICH *rushes out of the headmaster's office, followed by* ALEX.

ALEX: Dad, why did you do that?

RICH: The words just came out of my mouth.

ALEX: But . . .

RICH: I couldn't sit there a second longer hearing you lie on my instructions. Moore wasn't buying it anyway.

ALEX: I did my best.

RICH: Nothing wrong with being a bad liar, Alex. Nothing wrong.

ALEX: You stood up and said bullshit.

RICH: Did I? In front of the head?

ALEX: In front of everyone.

RICH *smiles, amazed by his outburst and pleased with it.*

ALEX: What's going to happen now? With your work.

RICH: I've blown it. Back at school, there were many Barkers. I kept quiet, never said a word, sucked it up – that's what a bursary boy does. Shuts up. Smiles. Must be grateful, always grateful. But not today. Today, Hobo Junior finally spoke out, and it felt flipping awesome.

ALEX *smiles, enjoying his father's (unusual) great mood.*

RICH: I should never have asked you to do that.

In a seamless transition to the home sitting room, LOU *joins them and embraces* RICH.

LOU: I'm so damn proud of you.

A rare moment of closeness between the couple.

RICH: The deal's finished, will never happen now.
LOU: There'll be others.
RICH: Not like this one.
LOU: Do you think Moore believed you?
RICH: He said he'd corroborate, that's the word he used – corroborate – with the other boys. I'm bullish about the outcome. Maybe this will swing it for Alex.
LOU: Can you imagine if Jules Barker is the only one expelled?
RICH: Imagine that.

RICH's *phone rings.*

RICH: Barker, seventh time he's called. [*answering*] Barker, fuck off.

Exhilarated, he cuts the call. They laugh. RICH *hugs* LOU *again. She leans her head on his shoulder.*

In his room, ALEX *records a voice note to* CASS.

ALEX: Hey Cass, it seems I might come back to school. This whole thing has been such a nightmare, like I tripped and fell down this mountain. There was no way out – until now. I can't wait to see you. I hope we can talk, find a way to being you and me . . . together.

SCENE 19

LOU and RICH are relaxed, sitting together on the sofa. LOU scrolls on her iPad.

LOU: Nine new friend requests, most of whom I don't know. How do they find me?

RICH: You don't accept strangers, do you?

LOU: I have requirements.

RICH: Like what?

LOU: We need at least ten mutual friends. If that box is ticked, I check their feeds to see if I want mine cluttered with their posts. If it's all about selling something or endless Bible quotes against pastel backgrounds, it's an instant no – delete, delete, delete. See here: Glen le Roux sent a request.

RICH: Who's this?

LOU: I don't know. Glen le Roux. I'm checking his feed . . . [*she looks at her phone*] Oooh no, very quotey. [*reading*] Choose love always. The sky is not the limit, your mind is. Some hearts understand each other – even in silence.

RICH: Kill me now.

LOU: No, no, no, sorry, Glen le Roux – delete request.

RICH: What do you like about Facebook?

LOU: There are things.

RICH: Name one!

LOU: I find out stuff.

RICH: Like?

LOU: The chilli crunch you love so much, Poppy's Facebook post.

RICH: Thank you, Poppy, and thank you, Facebook. That chilli crunch changed my life.

LOU: You love the chilli crunch.

RICH: I might have found it myself. In the shops? Like we used to?

LOU: Sometimes you need to know what you are looking for.

RICH: Hmmm, not sure the chilli crunch makes up for all the disinformation Meta spews. Number one place for radicalisation, sexual exploitation, polarisation, voter manipulation . . . but anyway, what else do you like?

LOU: Birthday heads-up.

RICH: That is useful. Anything uplifting?

LOU: I find links to music I might never hear.

RICH: And?

LOU: Keep up with old school friends. Nice to see their lives, their families.

RICH: Anything else?

LOU: I like to know whose parents have died. Facebook is very good for death. After a few hours, someone will say something, 'gutted', 'RIP', then I can send virtual hugs and show that I care.

RICH: Do you care?

LOU: Of course.

RICH: What if it's the death of someone you don't know?

LOU: I care that my friend cares.

RICH: Real friend or Facebook friend?

LOU: Both. Sometimes I think I know more about Facebook friends' lives than real-life ones. The other day, I bumped into Didi's daughter at the mall, and congratulated her on her dance show, she looked at me blankly, then

I realised I'd never met her, I only knew her from her mother's posts. Isn't that funny?

RICH: Not that funny.

LOU: Recipes! Sometimes I even make them. Well, I did once.

RICH: So, birthdays, recipes, strangers' deaths, and stalking old school friends.

LOU: You forgot the music.

RICH: There are better ways of keeping up with new music.

LOU: It's not all new. Chris shared a link to 'Don't Dream It's Over'. It took me back to the concert in London before we were married, when everything seemed possible.

They look at one another, remembering that time in their life. LOU *starts singing.* RICH *joins in with the chorus, followed by a pause as they keep looking at each other, filled with longing for the closeness they once had.*

LOU: When did we stop listening to music together?

RICH: Around the same time we stopped kissing.

Beat. RICH *presses play on his phone. Crowded House plays.* LOU *inches towards him. He puts his arm around her as they listen to the music, warmed by the nostalgia.*

SCENE 20

ALEX *flashes through a series of photographs of* CASS's *matric dance pre-drinks. She wears a long, revealing dress and leans into suited* Dylan. *The enlarged images snap up successively until they cover all the walls, surrounding* ALEX, *as if he is consumed by them.*

ALEX [*recording a voice message*]: Hey Cass, saw the photos of you and Dylan at the pre-drinks. You were all over him. What the fuck? You together with him now? Just don't tell Liyema what he calls his black friends behind their backs. Or Hales that he's a purebred homophobe. For fuck's sake, Cass. You don't belong with someone like that. You belong with me.

ALEX *presses send. He looks at the photographs again and zooms in on her face. The message gets blue-ticked. She's heard the voice note.* ALEX *notes her typing under her profile. He perks up, she's reaching out. The message is sent, visible on the screen/wall: Please don't contact me again. Desperate,* ALEX *records another voice note.*

ALEX: Cass, please, don't do this. I miss you. Sometimes it feels like I can't breathe, it's that bad. Call me, Cass, please.

ALEX *sends the message. The photos on the walls disappear one by one. He can't believe it.*

ALEX: She's blocked me! Fuck!

Beat.

ALEX [*recording a voice message*]: Hey Cass, it's me, your ex, Al-ex. You'll never listen to this because I'm blocked but I think you should know, I shared all the nudes to a big group of Chiswick guys. How does that make you feel? How does that feel? How does that feel?

ALEX *breaks down. He gathers himself and records another message, even though he knows she won't see it.*

ALEX: Even though you deleted us. Me. Block Alex. Delete Alex, like I never existed, like we weren't a thing. I'd never share them, Cass. Never. I've deleted all of them. I love you.

SCENE 21

RICH *and* LOU *talk to one another with equanimity as they face the practicalities of the situation.*

RICH: I've told a few placement agencies I'm open to offers.

LOU: I need to sort out the house before it goes on the market.

RICH: Maybe after Alex has written, wherever he writes, we can go away on a family holiday.

LOU: We can't afford to go away.

RICH: Somewhere nearby. Magaliesberg. What about camping? Mountain Sanctuary?

LOU: Maybe.

RICH: If you don't want to . . .

LOU: No, I do. I don't know what I want. I was driving the other day with the GPS telling me where to go, turn left, take the second exit from the next roundabout, no need to think. Just follow instructions. I thought how I'd love that for life. Buy chicken for supper. Love your husband. Hang the washing out.

RICH: You need help. I do like the love your husband part, but Lou, this online life of yours brings you down.

LOU: Not all the time. When I feel lonely, I dip in, find someone to connect to, it's comforting.

RICH: Why can't you do that with me? That's how it used to be, we'd talk, look one another in the eye . . . connect. Now every time I look at you, you're on your phone.

LOU: Sometimes it feels easier with people you don't know well.

RICH's *phone pings. He checks it.*

SCENE 21

RICH: The email from Moore arrived.

LOU: And?

> RICH *reads the email silently while* LOU *waits anxiously.*

RICH: Expelled!

LOU: No!

RICH: The stories clashed, the only unbiased evidence is in the video, they're all expelled. Including Barker, thank God for small mercies.

LOU [*rage building*]: They should use this to educate them – this is what happens when you make a mistake that is beamed to the world. I'm going to post something about how the school has failed these boys – 'Do not send your sons to Chiswick'.

RICH: Calm down. Do not post anything.

LOU: Alex won't cope. It's too much. He's a kind, sensitive boy, not the monster they're making him out to be. That's how he will be seen from now on. The guy who laughs at rape. And in the middle of all this, Cass dumps him! When she needed him, he was there for her, but when he needs her, she breaks his sweet heart.

SCENE 22

CASS *answers the video call from* LOU. *Her side of the call is projected onto a side wall.*

LOU *speaks directly to* CASS *on screen.*

CASS [*warily*]: Hello . . . ?

LOU: Cass, so pleased you finally answered.

CASS: I . . . I wasn't sure if you meant to call me.

LOU: This is no pocket dial, Cass.

CASS [*uneasily*]: But like did you mean to video call?

LOU: Oh yes.

CASS: Okay . . .

LOU: How are you, how're the studies going?

CASS: Fine, thanks.

LOU: Excellent. How was your dance?

CASS: Uh . . . okay?

LOU: So, you took Dylan Vermeulen? Saw the pics on Instagram. That was quite a dress. [*Beat.*] We bought a suit for Alex to match the colour of your dress. Absolute waste of money. Anyway, as long as you had a good time.

CASS: I'm sorry about the suit.

LOU: You know what I've been thinking about?

CASS: Uh, no.

LOU: When that holiday fling of yours told everyone you gave him a blow job behind the dunes in Plett. It wasn't easy having someone say that about your girlfriend, but Alex stood by you, didn't he, Cass?

CASS: Why are you doing this?

LOU [*losing any vestige of control she might have had*]: Just reminding you how lucky you were to have Alex. He's the best guy you will ever have. It's downhill all the way from here, my girl. Down, down, down. Alex is lucky to be rid of you. He can't see it and if you begged, he'd probably take you back ... in fact, that's what I'd do, Cass . . . beg him to take you back. Hopefully he'd say no, maybe now he sees that you're a little slut who gives it away to anyone anywhere . . .

CASS *cuts the video call.*

LOU: Cass, are you there . . . Cass? Cass!

LOU *throws the phone down.*

LOU: Bitch!

ALEX *enters, distressed.*

ALEX: Why did you do that?

LOU: Do what?

ALEX: Call Cass?

LOU: Just for a catch-up.

ALEX: You verbally abused her.

LOU: I did not.

ALEX: She recorded the call. She posted it on her close friends' group . . . they've all seen it.

LOU: She had no right to do that.

ALEX: You've made me look like some kind of idiot who gets his mad mother to fight his battles.

LOU: She hurt you!

ALEX: There is no way of me getting back with her now.

LOU [*desperately*]: I wanted to help. Show her she made a mistake. I had no idea she would record it.

ALEX: This is worse than being expelled. I hate you for doing this.

LOU: Don't say that.

ALEX: Dad's right, you live through other people. Through Facebook. Through me. You need to get a fucking life. Get out of mine!

ALEX *walks out.* LOU *is unravelling.* RICH *rushes in.*

RICH: You've lost it.

LOU *has a deranged look in her eyes as she paces.*

LOU: What's 'it'? Sanity? Decorum?

RICH: Your mind! Cass's father called me, threatening legal action.

LOU: He's a pompous prick.

RICH: Prick? You've never used that word in your life. Who are you? Where's Lou? You've lost her . . . down a spiral on Facebook.

LOU: Cass had no right to record me. That call was private.

RICH [*frustrated*]: Nothing is private! Nothing is private. Have you learnt nothing from this whole thing.

LOU: I hate Cass for what she's done to my child. I had to tell her that a little slut like her was lucky to have Alex.

RICH: She broke up with him, that's okay. It's allowed.

LOU: No! No! He's intrinsically good, and they don't see it. [*unravelling*] I hate Moore too. More. I hate Moore more. I'm so glad his wife has cancer.

SCENE 22

RICH: You did not just say that!

LOU *jumps onto the sofa.*

LOU: Oh yes, I did. Maybe I should post it. Yes . . . fuck you, Chiswick and Moore and Mrs Moore and Meta and Mark Zuckerberg! Fuck all of you for destroying my son's life. And mine. And mine.

LOU *starts to cry and slumps into the sofa.*

LOU: . . . and mine. And mine.

LOU *curls into a foetal position as she sobs.* RICH *moves in and embraces her tenderly. She quietens. Beat.* LOU *sits up suddenly.*

LOU: I'm going off Facebook!
RICH: Lou?
LOU: I swear I am going to.
RICH: Of course you are.
LOU: Oh God, I didn't mean it about Mrs Moore. Please, please pretend I never said that.
RICH: Said what?

LOU *folds into him, gratefully.*

LOU: You know what marriage is?
RICH: What?
LOU: It's a place where you can see the worst of someone . . . and still love them.

Music plays as LOU *and* RICH *cling to one another.*

SCENE 23

The music fades. Lights up on ALEX *on his bed.*

ALEX [*leaving a voice note*]: Liyema, please tell Cass I'm sorry. I need to talk to her. My mother's insane . . . she had no right. I need to talk to Cass. Tell her to call me. Thanks.

After covering LOU *gently with a throw,* RICH *moves across the stage and enters* ALEX*'s bedroom area.*

ALEX: Mom called Cass . . . verbally abused her!

RICH: Ja.

ALEX: As if things weren't already so messed up.

RICH: She loves you more than anything; she wants to protect you.

ALEX: She is way too involved in my life. She posts photos of me without asking, even if I say don't. I can't stand it. Plus, she takes the worst photos. The worst! Now this.

RICH: None of us has been our best selves. This video was a hand grenade thrown into our lives. We had no idea, no understanding of what it meant, how fast it would unravel, what to do, how to fix it.

ALEX: What if there is no fixing? Feels like everything is being destroyed . . . like I'm the worst person in the world.

RICH: People have done far worse and survived.

ALEX: But you've lost everything, and it's all my fault.

RICH: We all have lost things but found others. We're here for you, we need to support one another. Your mother just went about it in the wrong way.

ALEX: Deranged.

RICH: Possibly. Definitely. Temporary insanity, hopefully. I want more than anything for the three of us to survive this – together – and I think we can, as a family.

RICH *and* ALEX *are more connected than they have been; there's a softening in their relationship.*

SCENE 24

CASS *answers a Messenger video call from* LOU. *Both sides of the call are projected side by side onto the stage right screen.*

CASS: Leave me alone.

LOU: This is the only way I could connect with you.

CASS: I would have blocked you here, too, but I never use Facebook, it's for old people.

LOU: I'm also completely off it, but Messenger can be useful when you can't contact someone anywhere else.

CASS: Do I need a restraining order or something?

LOU: I was out of line. But seeing my child so broken . . . look, Alex loves you, for whatever reason, he does. Sorry, no, I didn't mean it like that. It's like I've forgotten how to speak. I should send you a message strewn with crying emojis, far easier. Cass, I'm sorry, so sorry . . .

CASS: Please don't apologise. It's embarrassing.

LOU: I am truly, truly sorry.

CASS: You said terrible things to me.

LOU: And you posted it. Can you delete that recording?

CASS: No!

LOU: Don't be angry with Alex. Please. He's furious with me . . . I . . . please delete . . .

CASS: I can't do this. I need to go.

LOU: Well, good luck with the exams . . . and if you . . . you're in the area, give me a call, we can have coffee.

CASS: Oh my God. You are insane!

CASS *cuts the call.*

LOU: I told Cass you had nothing to do with it. It was all me, in an unhinged moment. [*Beat.*] Everything got too much. Social media doesn't help, so I'm off.

ALEX [*incredulously*]: You're off Facebook?

LOU: Totally off.

ALEX [*suspiciously*]: So no social media.

LOU: Just a little Instagram, it's far lovelier, nothing too personal. I follow decor and travel and The Glucose Goddess . . . don't worry, I don't follow Cass or you. Or anyone you know.

ALEX [*laughing*]: Basically, you've switched platforms, owned by the same company.

LOU: Only for escapism. I never knew how invasive my thoughts could be.

RICH *enters, holding his phone.*

RICH: Who's Sizwe Ngubane?

ALEX: A guy who worked at Chiswick. Cleaner.

RICH: Mr Moore says he's come forward. Said Julius Barker was the one who made him buy the beers, not you. Sizwe has the WhatsApps to prove it. He saw Barker take the bag from Moore's car. Blew his story apart. Moore says only Barker is being expelled because he lied. The rest can come back to write.

LOU: Alex! At last.

RICH: It's all worked out.

LOU: The nightmare's over.

ALEX: I can't go back.

LOU: This isn't because of what happened with me and Cass?

RICH: It's only a few months, and you'll be done.

ALEX: You don't understand, Dad. I can't go back.

RICH: Why?

ALEX: I . . . I've posted something online.

Pause as RICH *and* LOU *absorb this.*

RICH: What did you post?

LOU: What did you post?

Lights down on the stage. ALEX's *post, filmed, appears on the centre wall.*

ALEX [*on screen, straight to camera*]: So what do we know about the esteemed Chiswick College? Boys to men. Well, there's the Hotties and Dogs app, designed by one of our boys. Rates all the girls at our sister school from the one you'd love to fuck to the one you'd rather die than fuck. So here it is, pictures of all the girls. [*Visuals of the app appear on the screen next to the image of Alex.*] Faces are concealed here, but not on the app. And the comments:

'I'd rather jerk off for the rest of my life.'

'She's a solid 5 – worth a blow job in the dark.'

'8 – she's hot, I'd fuck her all night.'

Here's one with woof-woof comments. Pics of dogs followed by vomiting emojis. Chiswick. Boys to men! Then, the head boy is a rapist. Fact.

It's hidden, but everyone knows. He's still the school's number one guy. First-team rugby captain. Leading the fucking way. Everyone knows he raped a girl at a party. Everyone. She was drunk, he dragged her off. She wanted to lay charges but his hotshot lawyer father stepped in and made it clear how he'd shred her rep if she tried. So yes, we were stupid arses but I want to stress this – no one was raped in that video.

Video ends. Lights up on ALEX, LOU *and* RICH *on stage.* LOU *sinks down.*

LOU: Oh God.
RICH: Why? Why?
ALEX: It's the truth, Dad.

Over loud music, snippets of the video of the mock rape, with ALEX, *on the side, laughing and clapping, play out over all the screens. More frames of the clips are repeated in blocks, emphasising the distressing actions.*

As the video fades, the family members are sitting apart, looking at their phones, their faces eerily lit by the phones' illuminated screens.

www.ingramcontent.com/pod-product-compliance
Lightning Source LLC
LaVergne TN
LVHW091307250826
846436LV00026B/280